# SAFE HANDLING OF BALES

GW01458343

HSE BOOKS

# FOREWORD

The Health and Safety Commission has endorsed the practical guidance contained in this document which it commends to the cotton and allied textiles industry.

# MEMBERS OF THE COTTON AND ALLIED TEXTILES INDUSTRY ADVISORY COMMITTEE

**Mr N F Swain**
Health and Safety Executive *(Chairman)*

**Mr P Booth**
Transport and General Workers Union

**Mr B T Bruce**
Cotton and Allied Textiles Industry Training

Organisation

**Mr D Duckworth**
Blackburn District Textile Manufacturers'

Association

**Mr B G Hazel**
Textile Finishers' Association

**Mr P F Hoggarth**
GMB - Clothing and Textiles Section

**Mr H Howorth**
Northern Counties Textile Trades Federation

**Mr P Jenner**
GMB - Clothing and Textiles Section

**Mr D Maloney**
Bolton and District Textile Employers'

Association

**Mr R G Morrow**
GMB - Clothing and Textiles Section

**Mr P J Perry**
Smith and Nephew Textiles Ltd

**Mr P Reid**
Transport and General Workers Union

**Mrs C Rudderforth**
Transport and General Workers Union

**Mr M A Sharp**
Coats Viyella Insurance Ltd

**Mr W Simpson**
Dawes and Co (Nelson) Ltd

**Mr R C Trotter**
GMB - Clothing and Textiles Section

**Mr P Williams**
Oldham and Rochdale Textile Employers'

Association Ltd

**Mr J Wilson**
John H Brooks Ltd

**Dr A Docker**
Employment Medical Advisory Service

*(Adviser)*

**Mr R E France**
British Textile Machinery Association

*(Adviser)*

**Dr M J Hewson**
British Textile Technology Group *(Adviser)*

**Mr D K Heseltine**
Health and Safety Executive *(Secretary)*

# **P**REFACE

This guidance booklet has been prepared by the Cotton and Allied Textiles Industry Advisory Committee (CATIAC) for the benefit of employers and employees in the industry. Advisory committees are appointed by the Health and Safety Commission (HSC) under Section 13(1)(d) of the Health and Safety at Work etc Act 1974 and form part of the Commission's formal advisory structure.

When preparing its work programme, CATIAC had identified a need in the industry for guidance on materials handling. The specific topic *Safe handling of bales* was selected for priority attention because a number of serious bale handling accidents, including fatalities, had occurred in recent years. A working group was set up to carry out the project and comprised representatives from employers, trade unions and the Health and Safety Executive (HSE). The guidance developed by the working group and presented in this booklet has been fully endorsed by CATIAC.

# CONTENTS

**1**    There is a long and continuing history of accidents in the cotton and allied textiles industry associated with the storage, transport and handling of bales.  Most of these accidents are preventable.  Resultant injuries range from the relatively slight to those involving serious, permanent disability or death.  The aim of this guidance booklet is to identify the relevant hazards and to recommend precautions and control measures to minimise risk of injury.

*Figure 1*
**Bales of fibre**

# SCOPE

**2**    The scope of the booklet covers two distinct activities:

(a)    the handling of bales of *fibre* (Figure 1) as encountered in raw and waste fibre spinning mills, and in warehouses and transport undertakings supplying such mills;

(b)    the handling of bales of *cloth* (Figure 2) as encountered in finishing works, and in warehouses and transport undertakings supplying such works.

**3**    Bales of fibre and bales of cloth can present their own particular handling difficulties but in most respects the hazards and the precautions required are the same. A common factor is the bale weight. Typically this is in the range 200-250 kg (4-5 cwt) but may be even more, up to about 350 kg (7 cwt).

**4**    There is an increasing tendency for cloth to be supplied to finishing works on pallets (deep pile plaited) rather than as bales.  For the purposes of this guidance booklet, cloth which is deep pile plaited (Figure 3) is regarded as equivalent to baled cloth since comparable problems arise.

*Figure 2*
**Bales of cloth**

# HAZARDS

**5**    Hazards commonly associated with bale handling and known to have caused serious injuries include:

(a)    dangerous manoeuvring and unloading of vehicles;

(b)    unsafe use of lifting equipment;

(c)    unstable stacking of bales;

(d)    poor techniques for manual handling;

(e)    unsafe bale opening.

**6**    *Safe handling of bales* places emphasis on these physical hazards, addressing the full range of precautions and control measures which are necessary. Health hazards are also considered where appropriate, for example the possible risks to health from exposure to cotton dust where cotton fibre bales are opened. Paragraph 103 gives an action check-list which summarises the guidance.

**7**    The booklet cannot address every conceivable hazard associated with bale handling. For example, new problems may arise as new techniques are introduced to replace more traditional handling methods. If there are doubts about the safety of a particular process or operation, further advice should be obtained from the equipment supplier, the relevant technical or trade association or HSE. Bale merchants and suppliers should also be called upon to provide appropriate safety information and guidance.

**8**    In some workplaces, because of local conditions or special circumstances, there may be a wish to adopt precautions and control measures other than those recommended in this booklet. Such initiatives are encouraged provided that they achieve at least an equivalent standard of safety and protection.

*Figure 3*
**Palletised cloth, deep pile plaited**

2

**9** *Safe handling of bales* is guidance, but it takes full account of relevant legislation, principally the Health and Safety at Work etc Act 1974[1] (HSW Act) together with various regulations made under that act[3-10].

**10** Some of the regulations of more recent origin[6-10] implement European Community directives on health and safety. These regulations are steadily superseding the provisions of pre-1974 legislation, for example the Factories Act 1961[2]. They also introduce various new requirements, notably the duty on employers to carry out risk assessments.

**11** The booklet addresses these legislative changes in a practical way but companies and individuals should keep abreast of developments through their legal adviser, their professional or trade association or HSE.

**12** For ease of reference, the main provisions of the HSW Act are summarised in paragraphs 13-15. More detailed information and guidance on the full scope of the current legal framework as it relates to bale handling can be found in the references[11-21].

# HEALTH AND SAFETY AT WORK ETC ACT 1974

**13** This act places a general duty on employers to ensure the health and safety at work of all their employees. The duty includes the provision of a safe working environment, safe plant and machinery, and all necessary information, instruction, training and supervision. Employers must also conduct their undertakings in such a way that people who are not their employees, for example contractors and other visitors, are not exposed to risk.

**14** Employees have a duty to take reasonable care for their own health and safety, must not endanger others and must co-operate as necessary with their employers on health and safety matters.

**15** Designers, manufacturers and suppliers of equipment for use at work must ensure that the equipment is safe and without risks to health. They must also carry out any necessary testing or examination, and provide the user with adequate health and safety information. These duties apply whether the equipment is supplied new or second-hand. For further information see HSE leaflet *Articles and substances used at work: the legal duties of designers, manufacturers, importers and suppliers, and erectors and installers*[31].

## PRE-EMPLOYMENT SCREENING

**16** Arrangements should be made for pre-employment screening to ensure that each person engaged in bale handling is medically and physically fit to undertake the work involved. Some tasks call for significant physical strength, and the temperament of the individual may also be important. For example, where teagling operations are carried out, the individual should be confident when working at heights. Further information is available in HSE Guidance Note MS 23 *Health aspects of job placement and rehabilitation - advice to employers*[30].

## INSTRUCTION, TRAINING AND SUPERVISION

**17** Safety in bale handling can only be achieved where adequate information, instruction, training and supervision is provided for all personnel involved in the work. The objective is to have personnel fully competent in the health and safety requirements of their job.

**18** Directors and senior managers, knowing that bale handling is a hazardous activity, should ensure that all necessary precautions and control measures are put into effect so that risk of injury is minimised.

**19** Supervisors should be fully conversant with safe working practices so that bale handling can be effectively overseen. They should be able to identify the training needs of the employees for whom they are responsible, ensuring they receive adequate information and instruction on the type of work they are expected to carry out. Special attention should be paid to younger workers whose over-enthusiasm and lack of experience can create additional risks.

**20** Personnel who use lifting and handling equipment should be fully trained in the safe operation of the equipment including any associated lifting tackle or attachments. They should have the ability to recognise a dangerous or potentially dangerous situation and take remedial action.

**21** Training of lift truck operators is particularly important. For new operators (those without lift truck experience prior to 1 April 1989) the scope of the training should cover that detailed in the Approved Code of Practice and Supplementary Guidance *Rider operated lift trucks - operator training*[11] and should include the passing of a test or tests of the skills and knowledge required. For operators who are more experienced, an assessment should be made of their skill and competence, and further training provided where necessary in accordance with the Supplementary Guidance. In all cases, conversion training is required for different types of truck or if unfamiliar lifting attachments are to be used. Periodic refresher training is also appropriate.

**22** Bales should normally be handled using mechanical equipment keeping manual handling on hand trucks to a practical minimum. Where manual handling cannot be avoided, personnel should be specifically chosen for the work and given training in the basic skills and knowledge required to move bales safely. This should be supplemented by detailed job training, adapted to the particular site and taking into consideration the weight, shape, size and density of the bales. Training should include instruction in the selection and use of the equipment such as hand trucks and hand hooks (Figure 4) needed to ease the manual handling operations.

*Figure 4*
**Hand truck in use, note assistance given by hand hook**

**23** General guidance on health and safety training in the textiles industry is contained in *Health and safety training and information pack*[36] compiled by CATIAC. Also relevant is HSC's *Policy statement on health and safety training*[35].

**24**    Lifting and handling equipment is involved all too often in serious bale handling accidents.  Common problems are unsafe operation of lift trucks, and dangerous slinging practices where lifting tackle is used in association with cranes or hoists.  Poor maintenance of equipment leading to mechanical failure is also a factor in some incidents.

# LIFT TRUCKS

**25**    Lift trucks are used extensively for handling and transporting bales (Figure 5). Some of the problems likely to arise, and the precautions required, are identified in paragraphs 26-34.  For more detailed guidance see booklet HS(G)6 *Safety in working with lift trucks*[22].

**26**    Lift truck safety problems include:

(a)    overturning, with or without a load, particularly if travelling at excessive speed or if manoeuvring over sloping or uneven ground;

(b)    collisions with pedestrians, the building structure or other vehicles;

(c)    instability of the load being carried;

(d)    unsafe practices such as carriage of passengers, or personnel riding on the forks;

(e)    poor or inadequate maintenance.

*Figure 5*
**Bale handling using lift truck**

**27**    Use of lift trucks should be restricted to operators who are trained and competent (see paragraph 21) and authorised in writing.  The operators should always be effectively supervised.

**28**    The rated capacity of a lift truck is usually associated with its  capability when operating on a firm, level surface with the mast vertical.  If sloping or uneven ground has to be crossed, the supplier or manufacturer of the truck should be consulted to ensure that the truck remains within its stability limits for the range of bale weights and sizes to be handled.  The effect on stability of any attachment mounted on the truck, for example squeeze clamps, should also be taken into account.  Derating may be called for in some cases.

**29**    The load itself should be stable, and the preferred lifting method is to use squeeze clamps with the bales arranged a maximum of two high. If forks are used and if it is judged safe to carry more than one bale at a time, the bales should again be arranged no more than two high. Loading any higher could easily cause the bales to topple and is not acceptable.

**30** In traditional buildings where the roofs are supported by cast iron columns, there is a significant risk of roof collapse if a column is struck and fractured by a truck. Columns in main driving areas should be clearly marked, for example with yellow and black stripes near eye level (Figure 6). Physical protection should be provided for slender columns in particularly vulnerable positions.

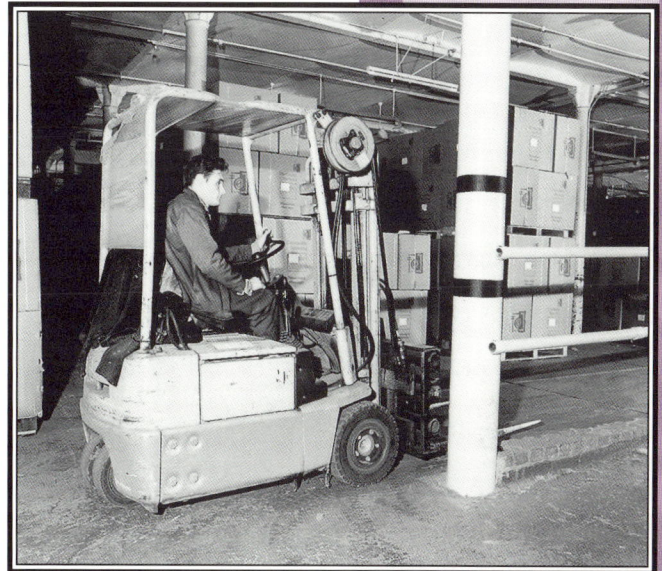

**31** A substantial overhead canopy should be fitted to the truck to protect the operator in the event of falling bales, or in the worst case, a roof collapse. Other fittings can be provided to reduce the probability of collisions but are not a substitute for proper care and attention by the operator. The fittings listed below are recommended:

(a) a horn or other audible warning;

(b) an amber flashing warning beacon;

(c) driving lights if the truck is used externally or in poorly lit conditions;

(d) reversing lights.

Note that rear view mirrors are not recommended.

**32** Lift trucks should be properly maintained in good repair with routine maintenance carried out in accordance with the manufacturer's schedule. It is usually appropriate for this to be done periodically according to hours run. Operators should also carry out daily checks and there should be a procedure for reporting faults.

**33** The load chains are classified as lifting tackle and must be thoroughly examined by a competent person at least once every 6 months (see paragraph 48). In addition, regular thorough examination of the whole truck is strongly recommended and can conveniently be carried out at the same time.

*Figure 7*
**No riding on forks! No standing under load!**

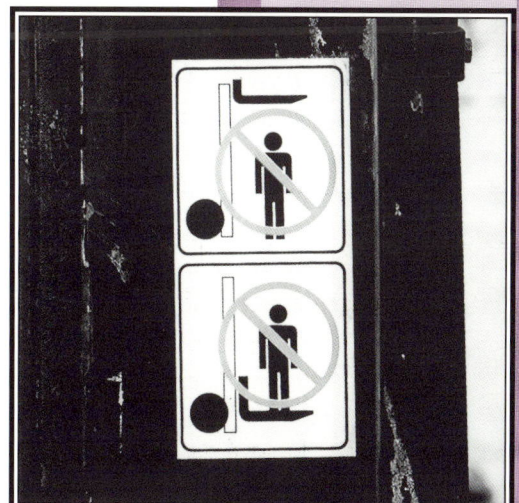

**34** If a lift truck is to be used as a means of access by fitting a platform, this is only acceptable if precautions are taken as described in HSE Guidance Note PM 28 *Working platforms on fork lift trucks*[25]. In no circumstances should personnel ride on the forks or on a pallet carried on the forks. Nor should they stand under the load (Figure 7).

# CRANES AND TEAGLE HOISTS

**35** Cranes and teagle hoists are sometimes used for lifting bales, particularly in older-type mill buildings. Possible safety problems include:

(a)   inadequate maintenance;

(b)   overloading;

(c)   other abuse or misuse, especially of the associated lifting tackle.

There is also a risk of people falling from unprotected teagle openings.

**36** Proper maintenance of cranes and teagles is important, with particular attention being given to the condition of the load chains or ropes. In addition, the equipment must be thoroughly examined by a competent person at least once every 14 months and a report obtained. Engineering insurance companies can carry out this work but it is the responsibility of the user of the equipment to remedy any safety defects.

**37** Cranes and teagles must not be overloaded and should only be operated by trained, competent personnel. The training should include detailed instruction in the selection, safe use and care of the associated lifting tackle (see paragraphs 40-49).

**38** Most cranes and teagles have point (or eye) load hooks from which the associated lifting tackle is suspended. In such cases, the fitting of a safety catch to the load hook (Figure 8) is regarded as essential to minimise the risk of accidental displacement of the lifting tackle from the hook.

**39** At teagle hoists of traditional design, there is a risk of people falling from the teagle openings if, for practical reasons, the openings cannot be protected by means of a safety bar or other barrier when the hoist is actually in use. The following precautions should be taken at each opening where a person could fall and suffer injury:

*Figure 8*
**Crane hook fitted
with safety catch**

(a)     provide secure handholds, one on each side of the opening;

(b)     keep the adjacent floor in good repair and free from anything likely to cause a person to slip or trip;

(c)     except when the opening is actually in use, keep it fenced off, as a minimum by means of a safety bar (a chain is not acceptable) but preferably by closing and locking the doors;

(d)     for any person who has to work at or near the opening when it is not fenced off, provide a safety harness attached by means of a lanyard to a secure anchorage (Figure 9);

(e)     ensure the safety harness and lanyard are used when necessary.

Inertia reel lanyards are available and can provide a high level of safety without unduly restricting freedom of movement.

*Figure 9*
**Safety harness in use at teagle opening**

# LIFTING TACKLE

**40**     Lifting tackle in common use in connection with bale handling includes:

(a)     chain slings, usually fitted with bale hooks or clamps;

(b)     fibre rope and wire rope slings;

(c)     webbing slings and roundslings.

**41**     If the lifting tackle is suitable for the job in hand and is properly used and maintained, few problems will arise.  Problems are much more likely if the tackle is abused or misused, or if it is unsuitable for the bales to be lifted.

**42**     Proper training for each person who uses lifting tackle is essential.  This training should include detailed instruction on the selection, safe use and care of the tackle. Guidance on safe use is available in *Code of practice for the safe use of lifting equipment*[37] published by the Lifting Equipment Engineers' Association.

**43**     Items of lifting tackle when not in use should be properly stored to prevent damage and to avoid tripping hazards.  Suitable wall-mounted storage racks or hooks located near the work area are recommended so that the tackle is conveniently accessible.

**44** Where multi-legged slings are used, personnel should understand how the safe working load decreases as the angle between the legs increases. Slings of sufficient length should be selected so that the angle made between the legs does not exceed 90°.

**45** To reduce the risk of multi-legged slings slipping from the load hook of the associated crane or teagle, the legs should join at a master link (or ring) which is itself suspended from the hook. Direct attachment of each leg to the hook is not good practice. See paragraph 38 concerning load hook safety catches.

*Figure 10*
**Bale hooks entered deep into hard bale of fibre**

**46** Bales of fibre are sometimes lifted using a chain sling fitted with a pair of bale hooks or clamps. Hooks are effective on hard bales, clamps are more suited to soft bales. A secure purchase should always be obtained on the bulk of the bale (Figure 10). Lifting on the bale wires or straps which could break is highly dangerous.

**47** An endless rather than a two-legged chain sling should always be used in conjunction with the hooks or clamps. This is because when a bale is lifted, the force in an endless sling causes the bale to be gripped more tightly whereas with a two-legged sling there is a tendency for the bale to slip through.

**48** Each item of lifting tackle, including the load chains of lift trucks, must be thoroughly examined by a competent person at least once every six months and a report obtained. Many users look to their engineering insurance companies for this service, but it is for a person such as the site engineer to ensure that any safety defects noted at the thorough examination receive attention.

**49** Despite all appropriate precautions being taken, it is still possible, if unlikely, for a suspended bale to fall. The bale could become detached from the tackle, the tackle could become detached from the hook of the associated crane or teagle, or there could be a mechanical failure of the equipment. As a fundamental rule, at no time should a person be in a position of danger beneath a suspended bale in case it does fall. Note that a falling bale, on striking the ground, could easily bounce sideways a considerable distance, perhaps 6 metres (20 ft) or so.

# L IFTS

**50**    Lifts are sometimes used for moving bales between floors.  Mostly they are of the electric traction type but may be hydraulically operated.  In some buildings, purpose-designed bale elevating systems also classified as lifts have been installed (Figure 11).

**51**    Proper maintenance of lifts is important with particular attention being given to the integrity of the gates, gatelocks and other safety devices.  There should be a fault reporting procedure, and a maintenance contract should be arranged with a competent firm of lift service engineers.  In addition, each lift must be thoroughly examined by a competent person at least once every six months and a report obtained.  Engineering insurance companies can carry out this work but responsibility rests with the user to remedy any defects affecting safety. Further information is given in HSE Guidance Note PM 7 *Lifts: thorough examination and testing*[23].

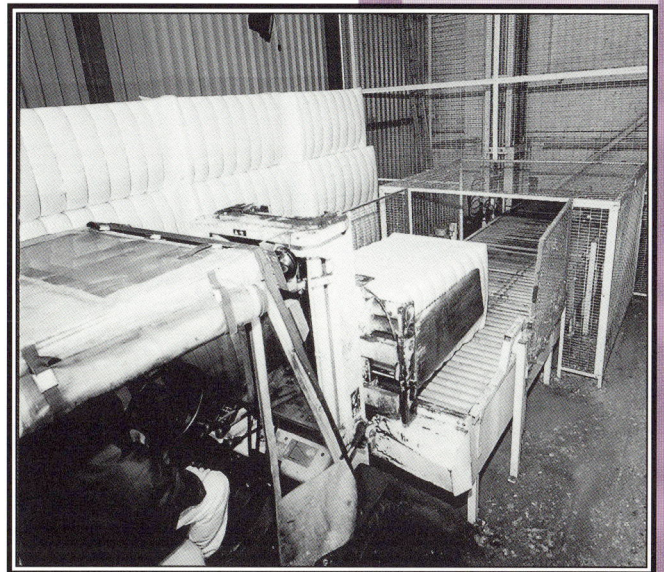

*Figure 11*
**Bale elevating system being loaded by lift truck**

**52**    Use of lifts should be restricted to authorised personnel, trained and competent in safe operating methods.  The safe working load should be clearly marked on the cage and must not be exceeded.

**53**    Heavy equipment such as power operated lift trucks should not be allowed to enter the cage.  Not only could this cause static overload of the installation but in all probability would also create excessive side force on the cage guides when the truck is braked.  Only hand trucks or small non-powered pallet trucks should be used for loading and unloading the cage.

**54** The proportion of road transport accidents occurring at industrial premises has increased steadily in recent years with operations such as loading, unloading and movement of vehicles (Figure 12) being the cause of numerous serious incidents.

**55** Transport safety depends to a large extent on safe operating procedures being devised to suit the individual circumstances of the site. The operating procedures should take into account the activities of the regular employees engaged in transport duties as well as the additional hazards introduced by visitors, especially drivers of delivery vehicles.

**56** A delivery vehicle when manoeuvring is extremely dangerous (Figure 13) and its movement should be strictly controlled. On arrival the driver should report to a responsible person and should be acquainted with any particular hazards or problems at the site. The driver should only manoeuvre the vehicle when authorised to do so by the responsible person.

**57** Risks from delivery vehicles and from internal works transport can be reduced by giving attention to the following aspects of traffic engineering:

(a) careful design of road layouts with a minimum of sharp bends and blind corners;

(b) pedestrians segregated from vehicles, and crossing places provided;

(c) one-way systems where practicable and the need for reversing minimised;

(d) spacious loading and unloading areas to avoid congestion;

(e) clear signposting, consistent with road traffic signs encountered on the public highway;

(f) good lighting in all operational areas.

Further guidance on transport safety is available in HSE Guidance Note GS 9(R) *Road transport in factories and similar workplaces*[26].

*Figure 12*
**A busy transport scene**

*Figure 13*
**Wagon drivers should beware of pedestrians**

**58** Problems associated with delivery and unloading of bales are addressed in paragraphs 59-78. During loading of bales, problems of a similar nature (but not specifically described in the guidance) can also occur, usually at the warehouses or transport undertakings where bales are made ready for despatch to the customer.

**59** Bales are usually delivered on flatbed wagons, in containers or in curtain-sided vehicles. Each delivery method presents its own particular problems during unloading. Safe working procedures should be put into effect so that unloading progresses in a planned, well-organised manner. Factors to be considered include:

(a) safe manoeuvring and parking of the vehicle (see paragraphs 55-57);

(b) with flatbed wagons, safe access to and working on top of the load;

(c) with containers and curtain-sided vehicles, safe opening of the doors or sides bearing in mind that bales, if insecure, could fall as the doors or sides are released;

(d) safe method of unloading, whether by lift truck, hoist and lifting tackle or by some other means.

*Figure 14*
**Typical flatbed wagon load**

# FLATBED WAGONS

**60** Use of open flatbed wagons is still a common method of bale delivery (Figure 14).

**61** Unsheeting and other work on the load may involve the risk of a fall. Where possible, the work should be carried out from ground level (Figure 15) by an experienced person such as the wagon driver. If the top of the load has to be reached, safe means of access should always be used, for example a properly secured ladder.

**62** Unloading by means of lift trucks is recommended

*Figure 15*
**Unsheeting from ground level**

13

(Figure 16). But if a hoist and lifting tackle have to be used because of the limitations of the site, see paragraphs 40-49. As stressed there, at no time should a person be in a position of danger beneath a suspended bale in case it is dropped or falls.

**63** A falling bale can bounce sideways a considerable distance on striking other bales or the wagon deck. In practice, therefore, it may be difficult for a person working on the wagon to obtain a position of safety as bales are hoisted. This problem could be avoided by firstly removing the bales from the wagon before making use of the hoist.

**64** Whatever unloading method is used, effective precautions should be taken to keep non-essential personnel well away, for example by providing barriers or warning signs. The whole operation should be properly supervised.

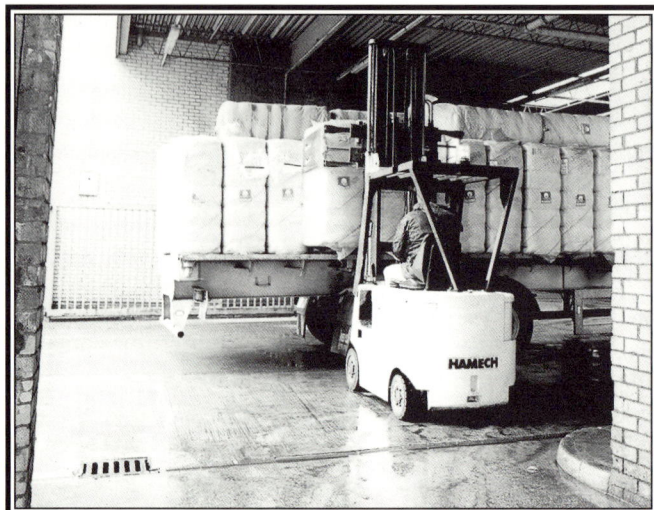

*Figure 16*
**Unloading flatbed wagon**

# Containers

**65** Containers nominally 12.2 metres (40 ft) or 6.1 metres (20 ft) long are frequently used for delivering bales.

**66** Most container vehicles are articulated and if the tractor unit is kept attached during unloading, application of the vehicle parking brakes should be sufficient to ensure stability. But if the tractor unit is detached for other duties, the semi-trailer and container assembly will be less stable, particularly when lift trucks enter the container to unload. In such cases the parking brakes should be applied and the semi-trailer supported near its forward end on purpose-built stands or jacks. To rely solely on the integrity of the semi-trailer landing legs is not enough.

**67** If the bales are closely packed and have expanded during transit, the expansion pressure within the container may cause the doors to be flung open

*Figure 17*
**Typical container load, loosely packed**

violently when the catches are released. A similar effect can occur if the load has been loosely packed (Figure 17) as movement of the vehicle may have caused the load to shift against the doors, leading to a risk of bales falling out when the doors are opened.

**68** To avoid danger when container doors are being opened, a lift truck should be positioned against the doors which can then be released in a controlled manner by slowly withdrawing the truck.

## *Loosely packed bales*

**69** The safest and most efficient method for unloading loosely packed bales is by means of a lift truck fitted with squeeze clamps entering the container from a platform or ramp, preferably a fixed ramp.

**70** Where a platform or fixed ramp is used, a dock leveller (Figure 18) or a properly secured bridging plate should also be provided to allow easy access for the lift truck into the container. Where a mobile ramp has to be used because of the limitations of the site, it should be fitted with effective means of anchorage to the container and the whole structure should be stable.

**71** Loosely packed bales carried in 6.1 metre (20 ft) containers can be unloaded by making use of tipping trailers which are available for this length of container. When tipping takes place, the centre of gravity of the vehicle is raised, increasing the possibility of overturning, particularly if the vehicle is jerked, thus tipping should only be undertaken in a safe area on firm and level ground. Personnel should be kept well away from the tipping area and the whole operation should be properly supervised.

## *Densely packed bales*

**72** With densely packed bales there may be unloading difficulties if the bales have swollen during transit and jammed tight. In this event, people should not place themselves in danger by attempting to manhandle the bales from within the container.

**73**    Jammed bales can normally be released by pulling, using a lift truck for this operation together with bale hooks or, in the case of bales of cloth, a webbing sling. A long rope or chain of adequate strength should be used to connect the hooks or the sling to the truck. Attachment should be to the towing eye of the truck and not to any part of the mast structure. The whole operation should be properly supervised with people kept well clear when pulling is taking place.

**74**    Where a rope is used for pulling, the material from which the rope is made should be selected having regard to the energy which is stored when it stretches under load. It is this energy which would be released and cause whiplash if the rope broke or if the hooks or sling became detached from the bale. Reputable suppliers should be able to advise on the selection and use of rope suitable for the given application.

**75**    As a last resort, jammed bales could be released by shunting, that is by opening and securing the rear doors of the container, reversing the vehicle and applying the brakes hard. But shunting should be avoided wherever possible, for the following reasons:

(a)    there is risk of damage to the vehicle and container assembly as it comes to an abrupt halt;

(b)    there is risk of personal injury as the bales are ejected from the container;

(c)    any bales remaining in the container may well be in an unstable condition and liable to fall.

If shunting is unavoidable and has to be carried out, the strictest supervision is required.

# CURTAIN-SIDED VEHICLES

**76**    Curtain-sided vehicles are increasingly used for bale delivery. The normal unloading method is by lift truck.

**77**    At the warehouses and transport undertakings where bales are made ready for despatch to the customer (Figure 19), the bales should be secured on the vehicle using the internal load securing straps (Figure 20). Otherwise, on arrival at the premises of the customer, there will be a risk of bales falling out when the curtain sides are released and drawn open. Customers should therefore have a clear policy on the standard of load security which they will accept, and should also adopt a safe working procedure for inspecting the bales before unloading.

**78** Despite the load security problem identified in the previous paragraph, unloading of curtain-siders is simpler in comparison with containers because of the ease of access through the curtain sides. In many cases the need for platforms or access ramps can be avoided. If, however, a decision is made to unload through the rear doors, the guidance in paragraphs 66-70 is applicable in relation to stability of the vehicle, safe opening of the doors and means of access into the vehicle.

*Figure 19*
**Loading a curtain sider**

*Figure 20*
**Tightening of curtain sider load securing straps**

# MECHANICAL HANDLING

**79** Once the bales have been unloaded from the delivery vehicle, they are moved either to store or direct to the process area. In many cases unloading and movement of the bales to their required location are combined as an integral operation using the same lifting equipment, for example where lift trucks are used.

# MANUAL HANDLING

**80** Some manual handling on hand trucks may be unavoidable (Figure 21) but should be kept to a practical minimum, particularly in view of the trend towards heavier bales. To ease the manual effort required, floor surfaces should be level, properly maintained and kept free from obstruction.

**81** Hand trucks of different designs and specifications should be available to cater for the various shapes, sizes and densities of bales. For example, trucks with serrated or spiked bases tend to grip well on hard bales whereas those with rounded bases are more suitable for soft bales.

**82** Single or multi-pronged hand hooks are sometimes used as an aid to bale handling. The hooks should be maintained in good repair and used in a way that ensures an efficient purchase as the bales are moved.

**83** Further guidance on manual handling is available in HSE leaflet *Getting to grips with manual handling: a short guide for employers*[34].

**Figure 21**
**Use of hand truck**

# BALE STORAGE

**84**    At most sites, bales are held in a warehouse or similar storage area (Figure 22) to await processing or despatch.  The primary safety objective in the storage area is to maintain safe and stable stacks so that bales do not fall.  Clearly, a bale is capable of causing serious injury or death even if it falls only a small distance.

**85**    Instability can occur in two ways:

(a)    stacks may be unstable from the outset because of poor stacking techniques;

(b)    stacks may have been stable originally but have become unstable, possible causes for this being: disturbance as adjacent bales are stacked or de-stacked; disturbance if struck by a lift truck; slippage of bales.

**86**    Avoidance of instability is not straightforward in practice due to variations in the shape, size, weight and density of the bales.  These variations call for stack configurations and methods of stacking and de-stacking which differ considerably from one bale type to another.  The surface texture of the bale wrappings is also significant.  For example, polypropylene and polyethylene wrappings are prone to slippage and can quite easily lead to instability in a stack.

**87**    An essential safety measure is to place the warehousing and storage operations under the direct supervision of an individual who is responsible, experienced and competent.  The individual, carefully selected by management and capable of making an objective assessment of the safety and stability of the stacks, should have the authority and personality to exert strict control over all aspects of the work.

**88**    Safe working procedures for stacking and de-stacking should be drawn up and agreed with all appropriate personnel.  The procedures should consider:

(a)    the limitations of storage area such as the floor space and height available;

(b)    the physical properties of the various types of bales (see paragraph 86);

(c)    the type of lifting and handling equipment to be used.

The need for stock rotation should also be addressed when optimising the stacking arrangements.

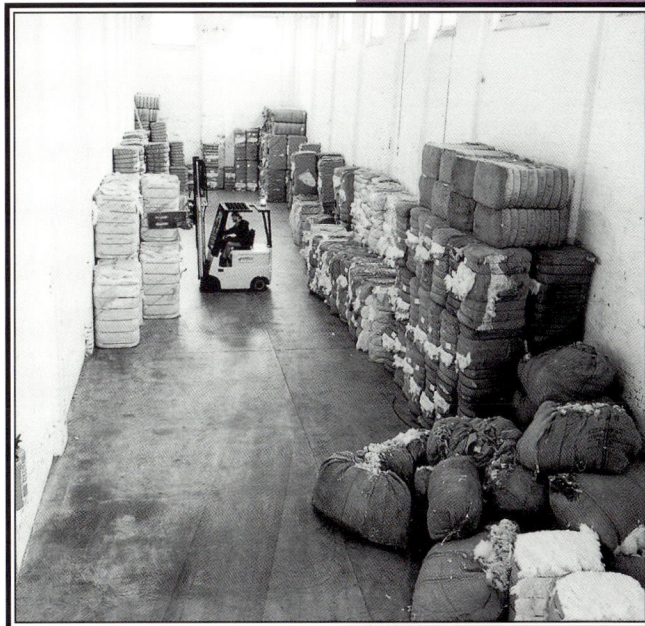

**Figure 22**
**Typical bale store**

**89** General pointers to safe practice are given below and should be taken into account when drawing up the stacking and de-stacking procedures needed at each particular site:

(a) clear gangways should be maintained within the storage area and between the stacks to permit safe movement of lifting and handling equipment;

(b) the surface of the floor should be firm and level, an uneven surface is not acceptable (Figure 23);

(c) the floor should not be overloaded, an important consideration in multi-storey buildings;

(d) stacking in pyramid fashion and using binder bales can help to stabilise the stacks;

(e) any damaged or otherwise doubtful bales should be stored separately, not in the bulk of a stack;

(f) no person on foot should be allowed near the stacks when lifting or handling equipment is operating;

(g) all stacks should be inspected at least weekly, with a record kept of the inspections and any resultant action.

**90** To minimise climbing on the stacks, any identification tickets attached to the bales should be positioned so that normally they can be read by a person standing at floor level (Figure 24). Where climbing is necessary on occasions for stocktaking purposes or for sampling, safe means of access should always be used, for example a properly secured ladder. Alternative safe means of access would be a properly designed and constructed work platform attached to a lift truck. See HSE Guidance Note PM 28 *Working platforms on fork lift trucks*[25].

**91** Bales are sometimes stored on pallets to facilitate handling by fork lift truck. Where pallets are used, the following additional considerations apply:

(a) the pallets should be suitable for the various types of bales encountered and should be boarded top

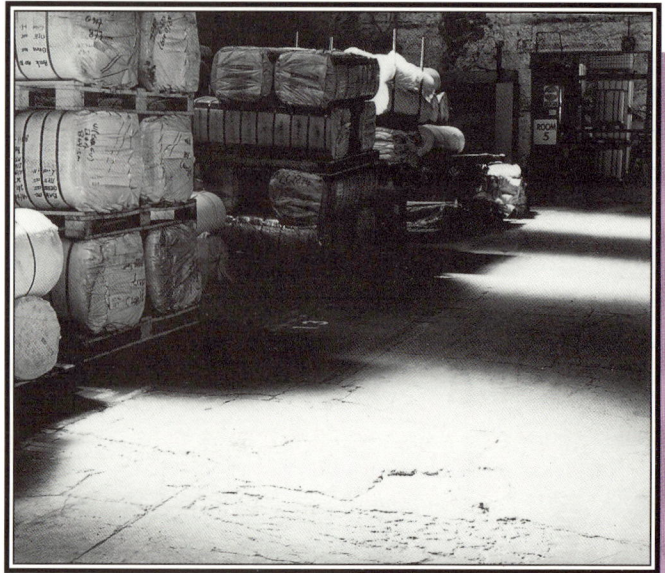

**Figure 23**
**Uneven floor in need of repair**

**Figure 24**
**Identification tickets positioned for easy reading**

and bottom to give extra strength and stability (Figure 25);

(b)  bales should be stacked on the pallets so that the forks of the lift truck give support to the full length of the bales;

(c)  stacks should not exceed 3 pallets high or 4.5 metres (14 ft 9 in);

(d)  any damaged pallets (Figure 26) should be withdrawn from service and either properly repaired or scrapped.

Further advice is given in HSE Guidance Note PM 15 *Safety in the use of timber pallets*[24].

Figure 25
A stable
palletised stack

Figure 26
Unstable stack on
damaged pallets

# BALES OF FIBRE

**92**  Bales of fibre are usually bound very tightly with metal straps or wires which are fastened while the bales are held under compression. Thus when the bales are opened, it is normal for the cut ends of the straps or wires to whip outwards.

**93**  Use of long handled cutters or axes (Figures 27 and 28) to cut the bindings reduces the need for close approach to the danger area and is preferable to using short handled cutters or hatchets. However there remains an obvious risk of injury, especially to the eyes. Each person at risk should be provided with and wear suitable eye protectors. Properly fitted full face visors are recommended. These are available with a curved portion under the chin which helps to prevent accidental displacement of the visor. Leather gauntlets should also be worn to protect hands and forearms.

**94**  Each binding is joined by a clasp, but the cut should not be made near the clasp which could so easily fly. Instead, the bale should be laid with the line of clasps held against the floor and the wires or straps cut along the opposite, upper side of the bale.

**95**  As successive bindings are cut, the tension in the remaining ones tends to increase. There is no specific cutting sequence which will prevent this effect although a sequence which promotes gentle expansion and barrelling of the bale is desirable. In any case there is always the possibility that a wire or strap will snap unexpectedly, hence the importance attached to the wearing of personal protection. All personnel not directly concerned with the work should be kept well clear.

**96**  Immediately after cutting, the wires or straps should be disposed of safely for example by placing in a skip. They should not be left on the floor (Figure 29).

**97**  When opening bales of raw or waste cotton fibre, there may be some risk to health from the dust given off and a risk assessment should be carried out as required by the *Control of Substances Hazardous to Health Regulations 1988 (COSHH)*[4]. Guidance is available in the following publications:

*Figure 27*
**Bale opening using long handled cutters**

22

(a)    HSE leaflet *COSHH: a brief guide for employers*[32];

(b)    HSE leaflet *Five steps for completing COSHH assessments*[33];

(c)    Booklet HS(G)97 *A step by step guide to COSHH assessment*[27].

**98**    The assessment should include measurement of the airborne cotton dust concentration in the workroom. See HSE Guidance Notes EH25 *Cotton dust sampling*[28] and EH40 (revised annually) *Occupational exposure limits*[29]. If the dust concentration is found to exceed the occupational exposure standard (currently 0.5 mg/m$^3$ total dust less fly measured by static sample) control measures are required to reduce personal exposure.

**99**    In practice a ventilated helmet respirator is likely to be a good solution to the cotton dust problem, if any. Such respirators, if properly used and maintained, not only give adequate respiratory protection but also provide the eye and face protection needed at bale opening.

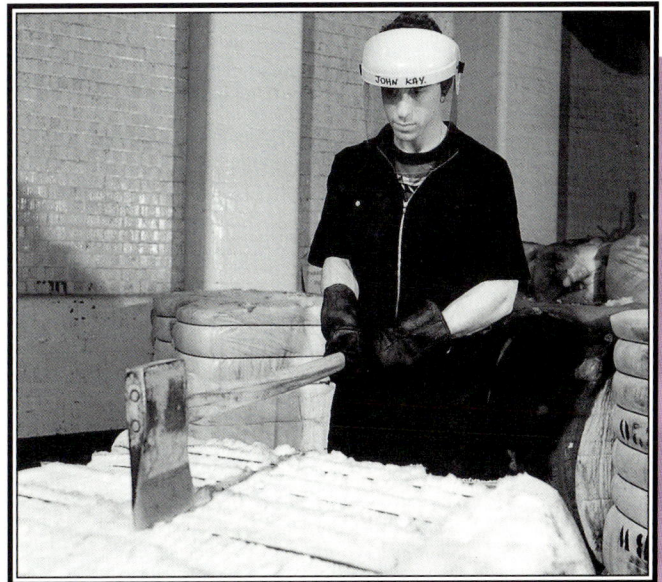

*Figure 28*
**Bale opening using axe**

# BALES OF CLOTH

*Figure 29*
**Bale wires or straps should not be left on floor**

**100**    Densely packed bales of cloth, protected at the corners with wooden packings, are usually bound tightly with steel straps. When opening such bales (Figure 30), the personal protection needed to prevent risk of injury from the straps is identical to that required when opening bales of fibre (see paragraphs 92 to 96).

**101**    Because of the wooden packings at the corners of cloth bales, there may be enough space for the bulkier jaws of special purpose safety cutters to be inserted. When safety cutters are used, the cut ends of the strap are restrained in the jaws and the tension in the strap is relieved as the jaws are opened. Risk of injury is somewhat reduced but the need for personal

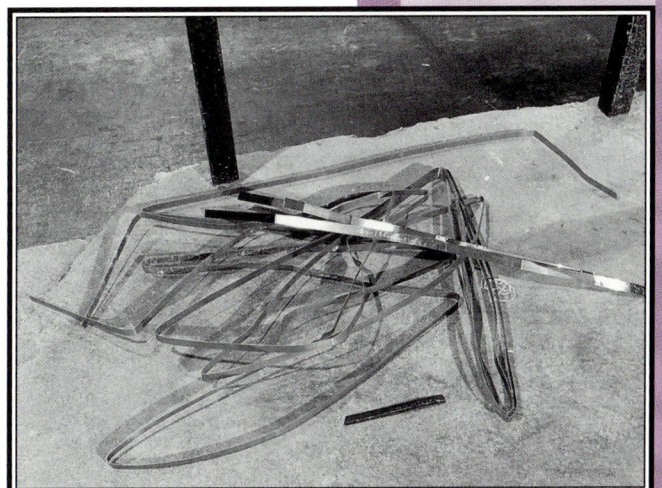

protection, especially eye protection, remains unchanged.

**102** Some dust may be given off when bales of cloth are opened but in most cases this dust is not likely to be in a concentration sufficient to cause a significant risk to health. In severe cases however, if a heavy concentration of dust is created, a risk assessment should be carried out as required by *COSHH*[4] and control measures applied as appropriate to reduce personal exposure. For guidance, see references [32, 33, 27].

*Figure 30*
**Opening bales of cloth**

**103** The action check-list below outlines a broad approach to implementation of the full recommendations contained in this booklet.

## GATHERING OF INFORMATION

Obtain and study carefully all relevant safety guidance.

Seek expert advice and assistance as appropriate.

## ACKNOWLEDGEMENT OF RESPONSIBILITIES

Acknowledge hazardous nature of bale handling operations.

Include section on bale handling in company safety policy.

Define specific areas of responsibility.

## SYSTEMS OF WORK

Review and make written assessments of all aspects of current systems of work including equipment used, transport, site layout, supervision, training etc.

Avoid need for manual handling where possible.

Lay down improved systems and procedures.

Highlight specific safety precautions.

## SELECTION/PRE-EMPLOYMENT SCREENING

Define job duties.

Check medical/physical/temperament fitness of employees.

## INSTRUCTION/TRAINING/SUPERVISION

Assess all relevant training requirements including supervision, operation of lift trucks, use of other lifting equipment, manual handling etc.

Produce detailed training plan.

Implement appropriate training.

Issue written instructions and procedures.

Test competency.

## LIFTING/HANDLING EQUIPMENT

Review suitability of all current equipment.

Consult suppliers and insurers.

Select equipment appropriate to usage.

Implement proper maintenance systems.

Ensure regular inspection by competent person.

## RELEVANT LEGISLATION

### *Acts*

1   *Health and Safety at Work etc Act 1974* Chapter 37   ISBN 0 10 543774 3

2   *Factories Act 1961*  Chapter 34 ISBN 0 10 850027 6

### *Regulations*

3   SI 1980 No 1471 *Safety Signs Regulations 1980*  ISBN 0 11 007471 8

4   SI 1988 No 1657 *Control of Substances Hazardous to Health Regulations 1988*   ISBN 0 11 087657 1

5   SI 1992 No 195 *Lifting Plant and Equipment (Records of Test and Examination etc) Regulations 1992*   ISBN 0 11 023195 3

6   SI 1992 No 2051 *Management of Health and Safety at Work Regulations 1992* ISBN 0 11 025051 6

7   SI 1992 No 3004 *Workplace (Health, Safety and Welfare) Regulations 1992* ISBN 0 11 025804 5

8   SI 1992 No 2932  *Provision and Use of Work Equipment Regulations 1992* ISBN 0 11 025849 5

9   SI 1992 No 2966 *Personal Protective Equipment at Work Regulations 1992* ISBN 0 11 025832 0

10   SI 1992 No 2793  *Manual Handling Operations Regulations 1992* ISBN 0 11 025920 3

### *Approved Codes of Practice*

11   *Rider operated lift trucks - operator training* Approved Code of Practice and Supplementary Guidance COP 26 1988   ISBN 0 7176 0474 8

12   *Control of substances hazardous to health and Control of carcinogenic substances* Approved Codes of Practice L5 (4th ed) 1993  ISBN 0 7176 0427 6

**13**  *Management of health and safety at work* Approved Code of Practice L21 1992

ISBN 0 7176 0412 8

**14**  *Workplace health, safety and welfare* Approved Code of Practice and Guidance

L24 1992   ISBN 0 7176 0413 6

## HSE PRICED PUBLICATIONS

### Legal guidance

**15**  *Guide to the Health and Safety at Work etc Act 1974*  L1 1990

ISBN 0 7176 0441 1

**16**  *Guide to the Factories Act (rev) 1961* 1991   ISBN 0 7176 0484 5

**17**  *A Guide to the Safety Signs Regulations 1980* 1981 HS(R)7

ISBN 0 11 883415 0

**18**  *Guide to the Lifting Plant and Equipment (Records of Test and Examination etc)*

*Regulations 1992* L20 1992   ISBN 0 7176 0488 8

**19**  *Work Equipment. Provision and Use of Work Equipment Regulations 1992.*

*Guidance on Regulations* L22 1992  ISBN 0 7176 0414 4

**20**  *Personal Protective Equipment at Work. Personal Protective Equipment at Work*

*Regulations 1992. Guidance on Regulations* L25 1992

ISBN 0 7176 0415 2

**21**  *Manual Handling. Manual Handling Operations Regulations 1992. Guidance on*

*Regulations*  L23 1992   ISBN 0 7176 0411 X

### Plant safety

**22**  *Safety in working with lift trucks* HS(G)6 1992   ISBN 0 11 886395 9

**23**  *Lifts: thorough examination and testing* Guidance Note PM 7 (rev) 1982

ISBN 0 11 883546 7

**24**  *Safety in the use of timber pallets* Guidance Note PM 15 (rev) 1993

ISBN 0 11 882161 X

**25**  *Working platforms on fork lift trucks* Guidance Note PM 28 1981
ISBN 0 11 883392 8

## Transport safety

**26**  *Road transport in factories and similar workplaces* Guidance Note GS 9(rev)
1992   ISBN 0 11 885732 0

## Health topics

**27**  *A step by step guide to COSHH assessment* Booklet HS(G)97 1993
ISBN 0 11 886379 7

**28**  *Cotton dust sampling* Guidance Note EH 25 1980   ISBN 0 11 883197 6

**29**  *Occupational exposure limits* Guidance Note EH 40 (revised annually)

**30**  *Health aspects of job placement and rehabilitation - advice to employers*
Guidance Note MS 23 1989   ISBN 0 11 885419 4

## HSC/HSE FREE PUBLICATIONS

**31**  *Articles and substances used at work: the legal duties of designers,
manufacturers, importers and suppliers, and erectors and installers*
Leaflet IND(G)1(L)REV 1987

**32**  *COSHH: a brief guide for employers* Leaflet IND(G)136L 1993

**33**  *Five steps for completing COSHH assessments* Leaflet PM(L)46 1993

**34**  *Getting to grips with manual handling: a short guide for employers*
Leaflet IND(G)143L 1993

**35**  *Policy statement on health and safety training* Leaflet IND(G)106(L) 1992

**36**  *Health and safety training and information pack* Cotton and Allied Textiles
Industry Advisory Committee Loose-leaf package IAC(L)61  1992

## OTHER GUIDANCE

**37**  *Code of practice for the safe use of lifting equipment* 3rd ed 1991 Lifting Equipment Engineers' Association Loose-leaf manual

## AVAILABILITY

HMSO publications (references 1-10) are available from HMSO Bookshops (see Yellow Pages) and through most good booksellers.

HSC/HSE priced publications (references 11-30) and HSC/HSE free publications (references 31 to 36) are available (mail order only) from HSE Books, PO Box 1999, Sudbury, Suffolk CO10 6FS (Tel: 0787 881165 Fax: 0787 313995).

HSC/HSE priced publications (references 11-30) are also available from Dillons Bookstores or can be ordered at any branch of Ryman the Stationer (see Yellow Pages or telephone 071 434 3000 for local details).

Reference 37 is available from the Lifting Equipment Engineers' Association, Waggoners Court, The Street, Manuden, Bishop's Stortford, Hertfordshire CM23 1DW (Tel: 0279 816504).

Printed and published by the Health and Safety Executive C25 6/94

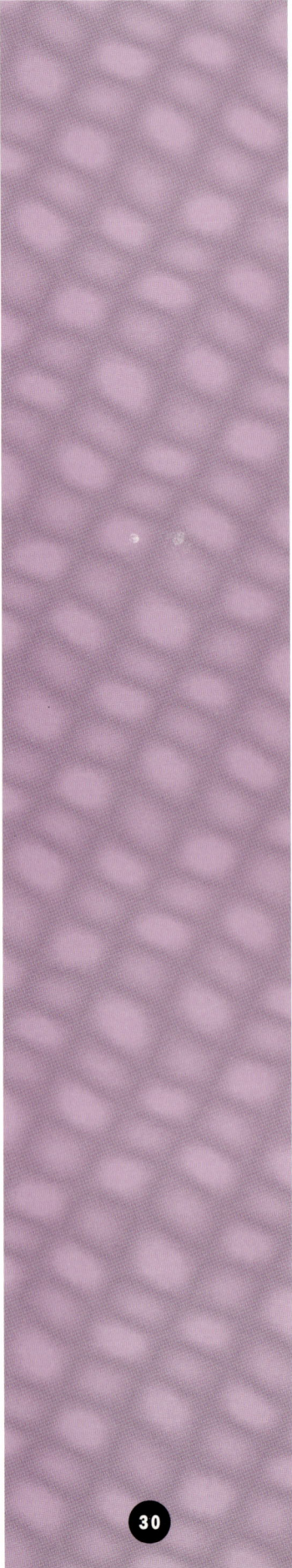